Alfred's Basic Piano Library

Popular Hits • Level 3

P i a n o

Arranged by Tom Gerou

This series offers Broadway, pop, and movie music arrangements to be used as supplementary pieces for students. Soon after beginning piano study, students can play attractive versions of favorite classics, as well as the best-known popular music of today.

This book is correlated page-by-page with Lesson Book 3 of *Alfred's Basic Piano Library*; pieces should be assigned based on the instructions in the upper-right corner of the title page of each piece in *Popular Hits*. Since the melodies and rhythms of popular music do not always lend themselves to precise grading, you may find that these pieces are sometimes a little longer and more difficult than the corresponding pages in the Lesson Book. The teacher's judgment is the most important factor in deciding when to assign each arrangement.

When the books in the *Popular Hits* series are assigned in conjunction with the Lesson Books, these appealing pieces reinforce new concepts as they are introduced. In addition, the motivation the music provides could not be better. The emotional satisfaction that students receive from mastering each song increases their enthusiasm to begin the next one.

No part of this book shall be reproduced, arranged, adapted, recorded, publicly performed, stored in a retrieval system, or transmitted by any means without written permission from the publisher. In order to comply with copyright laws, please apply for such written permission and/or license by contacting the publisher at alfred.com/permissions.

Produced by
Alfred Music
P.O. Box 10003
Van Nuys, CA 91410-0003
alfred.com

ISBN-10: 1-4706-2738-8
ISBN-13: 978-1-4706-2738-6

Cover Photos: Music speakers: © Shutterstock.com / Martin M303 • Headphones: © Shutterstock.com / Jiri Hera

What Do You Mean?

*Use with Alfred's Basic Piano Library,
Lesson Book 3, after pages 8–9.*

Words and Music by Mason Levy,
Justin Bieber and Jason Boyd
Arr. by Tom Gerou

© 2015 ARTIST PUBLISHING GROUP WEST, MASON LEVY PRODUCTIONS, BIEBER TIME PUBLISHING and POO BZ PUBLISHING INC.
All Rights on behalf of ARTIST PUBLISHING GROUP WEST and MASON LEVY PRODUCTIONS Administered by WB MUSIC CORP.
All Rights Reserved

Use after pages 14–15.

See You Again

(from *Furious 7*)

Words and Music by
Cameron Thomaz, Charlie Puth,
Andrew Cedar and Justin Franks

Arr. by Tom Gerou

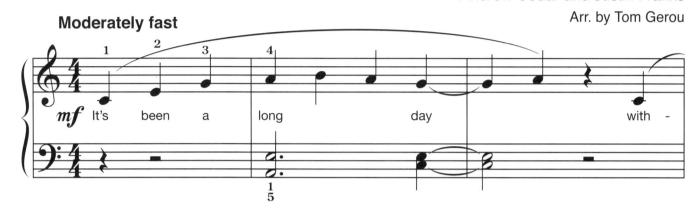

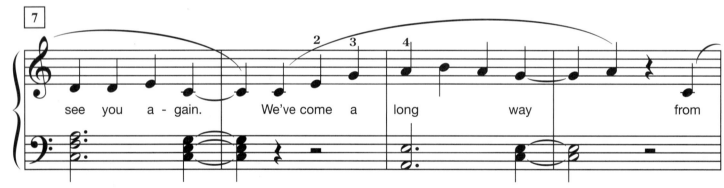

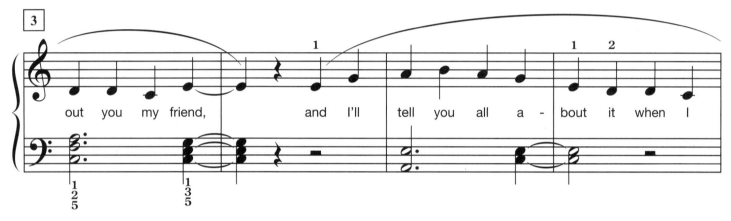

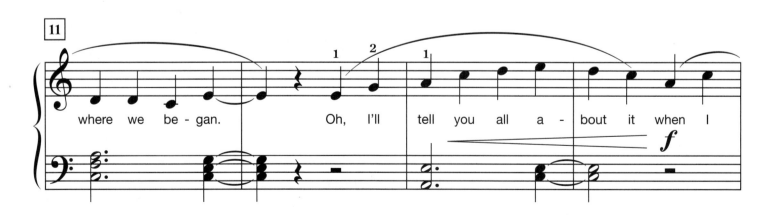

© 2015 WARNER-TAMERLANE PUBLISHING CORP., WIZ KHALIFA PUBLISHING, CHARLIE PUTH MUSIC PUBLISHING, ARTIST 101 PUBLISHING GROUP,
J FRANKS PUBLISHING, ANDREW CEDAR PUBLISHING, ARTIST PUBLISHING GROUP WEST, U.P.G. MUSIC PUBLISHING and
UNIVERSAL PICTURES MUSIC All Rights on behalf of Itself, WIZ KHALIFA PUBLISHING, CHARLIE PUTH MUSIC PUBLISHING and
ARTIST 101 PUBLISHING GROUP Administered by WARNER-TAMERLANE PUBLISHING CORP. All Rights for J FRANKS PUBLISHING,
ANDREW CEDAR PUBLISHING and ARTIST PUBLISHING GROUP WEST Administered by WB MUSIC CORP. All Rights for U.P.G. MUSIC PUBLISHING
Administered by SONGS OF UNIVERSAL, INC. All Rights Reserved

Use after pages 16–17.

The Big Bang Theory
(Main Title)

Words and Music by Ed Robertson
Arr. by Tom Gerou

Moderately fast

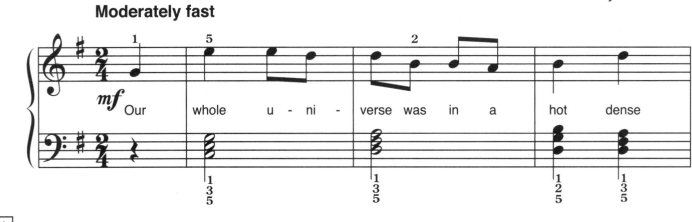

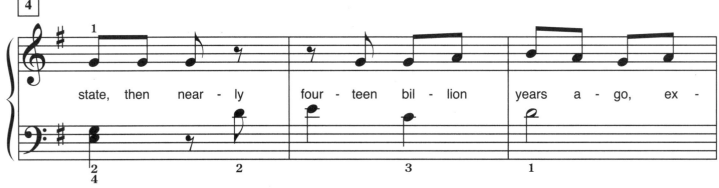

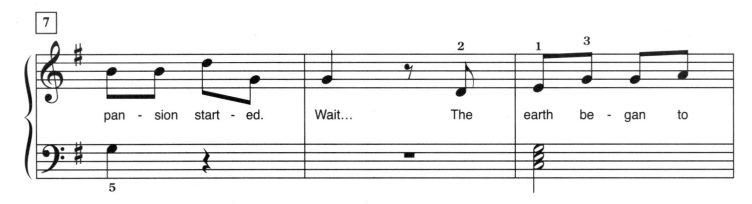

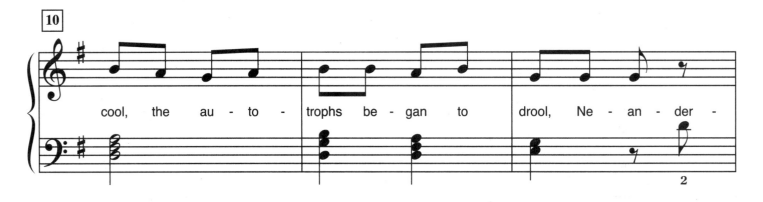

© 2007 WARNER-OLIVE MUSIC LLC (ASCAP)
All Rights Administered by UNIVERSAL MUSIC CORP. (ASCAP)
Exclusive Worldwide Print Rights Administered by ALFRED MUSIC
All Rights Reserved

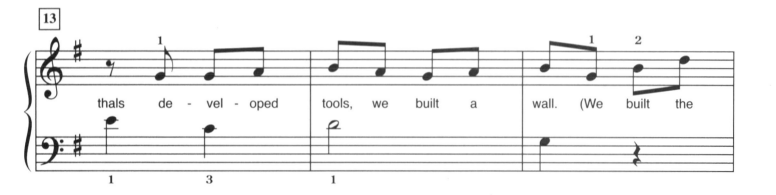

thals de - vel - oped tools, we built a wall. (We built the

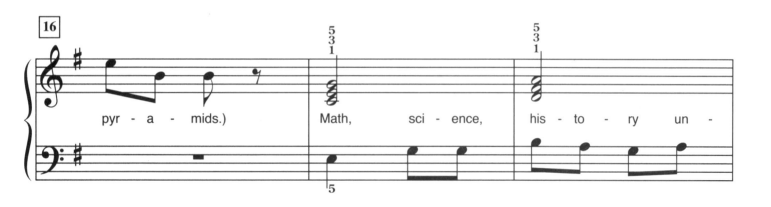

pyr - a - mids.) Math, sci - ence, his - to - ry un -

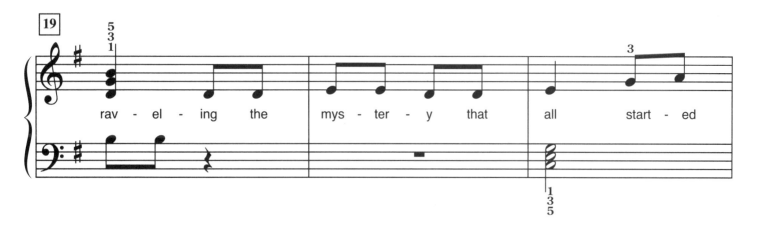

rav - el - ing the mys - ter - y that all start - ed

with the big bang!

Use after page 21.

You're Never Fully Dressed without a Smile

(from *Annie*—2014 Film Version)

Words and Music by Charles Strouse,
Martin Charnin, Greg Kurstin,
Sia Furler and Will Gluck

Arr. by Tom Gerou

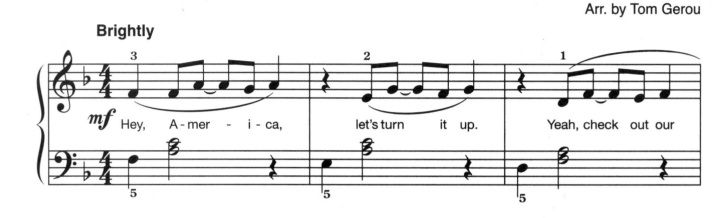

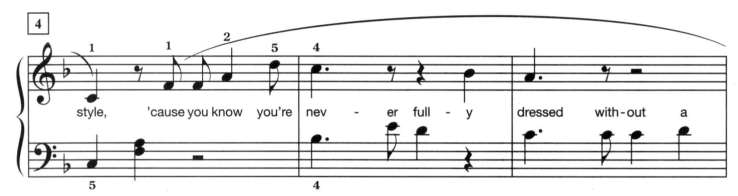

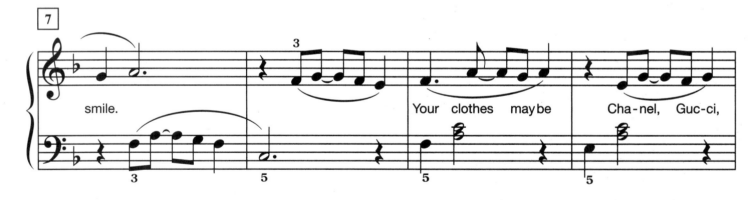

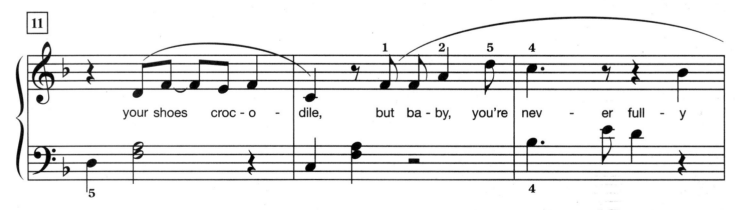

© 2014 CHARLES STROUSE PUBLISHING, EDWIN H. MORRIS & CO., INC., a Division of MPL MUSIC PUBLISHING, INC., EMI APRIL MUSIC, INC. and
SONY/ATV MUSIC PUBLISHING LLC All Rights for CHARLES STROUSE PUBLISHING Administered by WB MUSIC CORP. All Rights Reserved

Use after page 27.

When She Loved Me

(from Walt Disney's *Toy Story 2*)

Words and Music by Randy Newman

Arr. by Tom Gerou

Tenderly

When some - bod - y loved me, ev - 'ry - thing was beau - ti - ful.

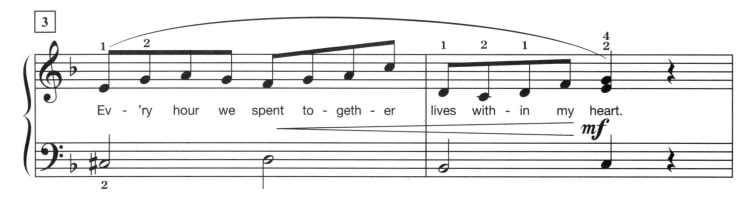

Ev - 'ry hour we spent to - geth - er lives with - in my heart.

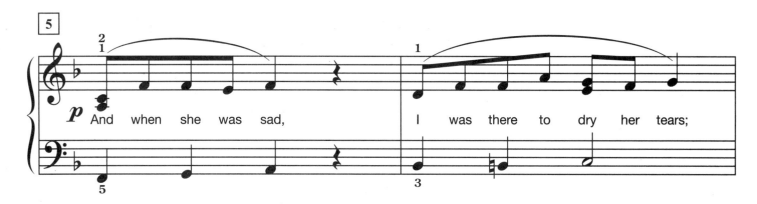

And when she was sad, I was there to dry her tears;

and when she was hap - py, so was I, when she loved me.

© 1999 WALT DISNEY MUSIC COMPANY and PIXAR TALKING PICTURES
All Rights Administered by WALT DISNEY MUSIC COMPANY
All Rights Reserved

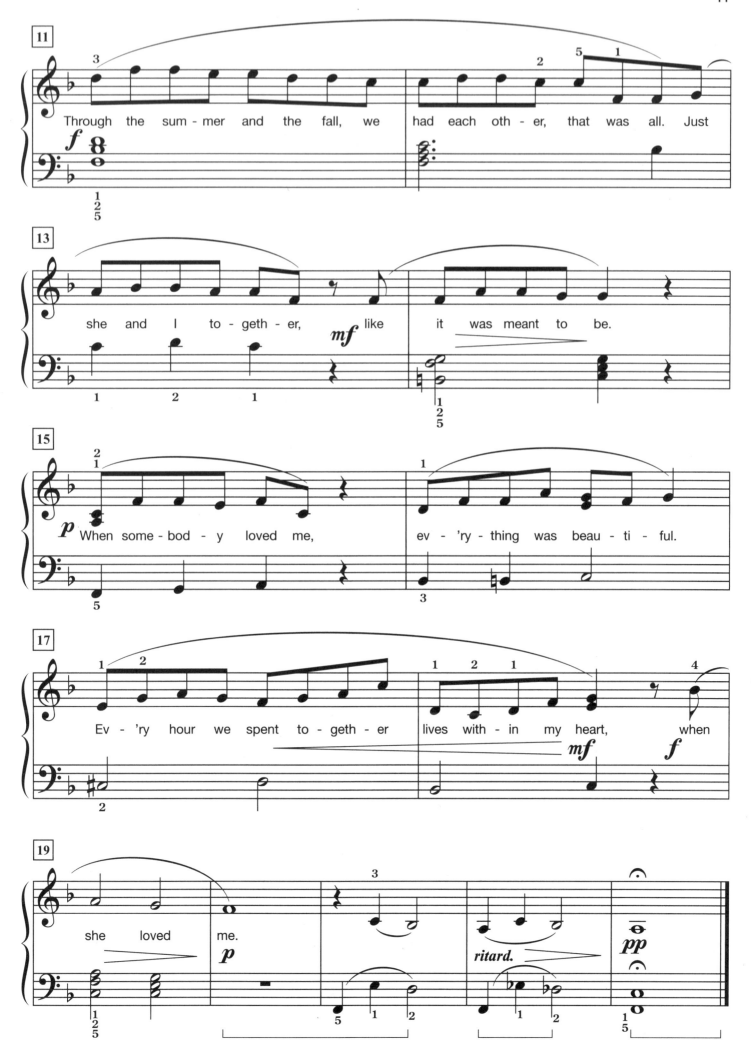

Use after pages 30–31.

Hedwig's Theme

(from *Harry Potter and the Sorcerer's Stone*)

By **JOHN WILLIAMS**

Arr. by Tom Gerou

© 2002 WARNER-BARHAM MUSIC LLC (BMI)
All Rights (Excluding Print) Administered by SONGS OF UNIVERSAL (BMI)
Exclusive Worldwide Print Rights Administered by ALFRED MUSIC
All Rights Reserved

Use after page 35.

Flicker
(Kanye West Rework)

Words and Music by
Mike Dean, Ella Yelich-O'Connor,
Noah Goldstein and Kanye West

Arr. by Tom Gerou

© 2014 WARNER-TAMERLANE PUBLISHING CORP., PAPA GEORGE MUSIC, EMI MUSIC PUBLISHING AUSTRALIA PTY LTD, NOAH GOLDSTEIN MUSIC and PLEASE GIMME MY PUBLISHING INC. All Rights on behalf of Itself and PAPA GEORGE MUSIC Administered by WARNER-TAMERLANE PUBLISHING CORP.
All Rights Reserved

Use after page 39.

Run with the Herd

(from Walt Disney Pictures' *The Good Dinosaur*—A Pixar Film)

By Mychael Danna and Jeff Danna

Arr. by Tom Gerou

© 2015 WONDERLAND MUSIC COMPANY and PIXAR MUSIC
All Rights Reserved Used by Permission

Use after pages 40–41.

James Bond Theme

By Monty Norman

Arr. by Tom Gerou

© 1962 UNITED ARTISTS MUSIC LTD.
Copyright Renewed by EMI UNART CATALOG, INC.
Exclusive Print Rights Controlled and Administered by ALFRED MUSIC
All Rights Reserved

Use after pages 44–45.

Colour My World

Words and Music by James Pankow
Arr. by Tom Gerou

© 1970 (Renewed) SPIRIT CATALOG HOLDINGS, S.à.r.l. and PRIMARY WAVE MUSIC PANKOW SPECIAL ACCOUNT (c/o Wixen Music Publishing, Inc.)
US, UK and Canadian Rights for SPIRIT CATALOGUE HOLDINGS, S.à.r.l. Controlled and Administered by SPIRIT TWO MUSIC, INC. (ASCAP)
Rights for the Rest of World are Controlled and Administered by SPIRIT SERVICES HOLDINGS, S.à.r.l. on behalf of SPIRIT CATALOGUE HOLDINGS, S.à.r.l.
All Rights Reserved